Ruth Bell Graham's
Collected Poems

Ruth Bell Graham's
Collected Poems

Ruth Bell Graham

BakerBooks
A Division of Baker Book House Co
Grand Rapids, Michigan 49516

© 1977, 1992, 1997, 1998 by Ruth Bell Graham

Published by Baker Books
a division of Baker Book House Company
P.O. Box 6287, Grand Rapids, MI 49516-6287

Printed in the United States of America

Library of Congress Cataloging-in-Publication Data

Graham, Ruth Bell.
    [Poems. Selections]
    Ruth Bell Graham's collected poems / Ruth Bell Graham.
       p. cm.
    ISBN 0-8010-1138-8 (cloth)
    1. Christian poetry, American. I. Title.
    PS3557.R222A6   1997
    811'.54–dc21   97-33544

For current information about all releases from Baker Book House, visit our web site:
                            http://www.bakerbooks.com

These are for
YOU

By way of explanation

As I wrote in *Sitting by My Laughing Fire* in 1977, I am, obviously, not a true poet, and these poems were never written for publication. Primarily, I wrote them for myself. I've written because, at times, I had to. It was write, or develop an ulcer. I chose to write. At times I wrote for sheer fun.

I have not included every poem previously published in *Sitting by My Laughing Fire* or *Clouds Are the Dust of His Feet*. But I have added many more. For your sake, not all are included.

I separated some early ones into small categories at the beginning (Childhood in China and High School in Korea, College and Early Love Poems, and Marriage and Motherhood).

Many of these poems were written concerning people or situations about which I felt deeply. Not all poems are autobiographical by any means. Those written for or about certain people, I have chosen not to identify so that you may read into them whatever meets you where you are.

These, you might say, are merely the footprints of a pilgrim.

Ruth Bell Graham
Little Piney Cove
Montreat, North Carolina
May 8, 1997

He sang atop the old split rail
all while it thundered,
raindrops pelting him like hail,
and, I wondered:

How one small, vulnerable bird,
defying deafening thunder,
could make itself so sweetly heard.
And still I wonder.

or as my publisher and agent might say,

How one small, vulnerable bird,
defying deafening thunder,
could make itself so annoyingly heard . . .
and heard . . .
and heard. . . .

Childhood in China
and High School in Korea

$\mathscr{L}$ook o'er the fields about you—
riveted, hilléd with graves;
no one can count the number
of those who perished as slaves;
slaves to the sin they were born in,
knowing not God or His Light;
died without God's great salvation,
died in the darkness of night.

Look o'er the people about you—
faces so furrowed with care,
lined and hardened by sorrow
sin has placed on them there;
think of the evil they live in,
hopes none and joys so few;
love them, pray for them, win them,
lest they should perish, too.

In as much" a cup of water
   offered one in Jesus' name,
"In as much" a gentle handclasp
   treating one and all the same,
"In as much" a single penny
   dropped in some poor beggar's palm,
"In as much" a piece of clothing
   just to keep a body warm,
"In as much," so said the Master
   (though the very least he be),
"In as much as you have done it,
   you have done it unto Me."

It isn't your gold or silver,
your talents great or small,
your voice, or your gift of drawing,
or the crowd you go with at all;
it isn't your friends or pastimes,
your looks or your clothes so gay;
it isn't your home or family,
or even the things that you say;
it isn't your choice of amusements,
it isn't the life you lead,
it isn't the thing you prize the most,
or the books you like to read;
no, it isn't the things you have, dear,
or the things you like to do,
the Master is searching deeper . . .
He seeks not yours, but you.

It's your heart that Jesus longs for;
your will to be made His own,
with self on the cross forever,
and Jesus alone on the throne.

Lord, when my soul is weary
and my heart is tired and sore,
and I have that failing feeling
that I can't take any more;
then let me know the freshening
found in simple, childlike prayer,
when the kneeling soul knows surely
that a listening Lord is there.

$\mathcal{N}$ow unto Him Who is able
spotless to keep His own,
presenting each ransomed sinner
blameless before the throne,
to the only wise God, our Father,
to Him Whom we all adore,
be glory, dominion, and power
both now and forevermore.

Like a shadow declining
swiftly away . . . away . . .
like the dew of the morning
gone with the heat of the day;
like the wind in the treetops,
like a wave of the sea,
so are our lives on earth when seen
in the light of eternity.

Spare not the pain
   though the way I take
be lonely and dark,
   though the whole soul ache,
for the flesh must die
   though the heart may break.
Spare not the pain, oh,
   spare not the pain.

Test me, Lord, and give me strength
to meet each test
unflinching, unafraid;
not striving nervously to do my best,
not self-assured, or careless as in
jest,
but with Your aid.

Purge me, Lord, and give me grace to
bear the heat
of cleansing flame;
not bitter at my lowly lot, but mete
to bear my share of suffering and keep
sweet,
in Jesus' Name.

Teach me contentment, Lord, whate'er my lot,
   keeping my eyes on You in trust,
   knowing Your love is true, Your way is just.

Teach discontentment, Lord, with what I am;
   daily striving, growing daily nearer,
   finding You are daily closer, dearer.

Contented, Lord, yet discontented make me,
   both together working, blending
   all in Your own glory ending.

*W*hen we come to know Jesus as Savior
and accept Him as master as well,
He is more than anyone told us,
and more than we ever can tell.

he LORD shall fight for you, and you
shall hold your peace."
Look up, O you of little faith;
let doubting cease.
The battle is the Lord's; He works
in a mysterious way.
'Tis not by might, nor power, but see
His spirit move today.
Unprofitable servants we;
our duty done, we must
look to Him for victory.
So . . .
be still, and trust.

The future is a blank without a view.
That which I wanted most, You have denied;
I cannot understand (and I have tried);
there's nothing I can do but wait on You.

Earth offered much, and I had, lingering long
outside her lighted windows, wistful grown—
till at my side I heard a voice—Your own.
Lord, how could I resist a love so strong?

Take all away. I am content to know
such love is mine—for life is all too brief
to grieve for pleasures bringing only grief;
give me but You; it is enough just so.

Enough—and more! Such love for You keeps growing—
in You I find my deepest joy complete,
all longing satisfied, and pain made sweet;
in You my cup is filled to overflowing.

$\mathcal{L}$ay them quietly at His feet
   one by one:
each desire, however sweet,
   just begun;
dreams still hazy, growing bright;
hope just poised, winged for flight;
all your longing each delight—
   every one.

At His feet and leave them there,
   never fear;
every heartache, crushing care—
   trembling tear;
you will find Him always true,
men may fail you, friends be few,
He will prove Himself to you
   far more dear.

Psalm 61:2

So helpless a thing my heart
    —and, oh, so small—
all overwhelmed, it looks to You for strength,
    nor looks in vain;
long it has struggled on, and now at length
    is crushed again.

Eager with expectation, rising
    but to fall,
wearily it longs for that great Rock
    "higher than I,"
where, with Your strength absorbing every shock,
    calm shall I lie.

There are no depths
    to which I have gone
or to which I could go,
    but Thou, in Thy fathomless
mercy and love
    didst still sink below,
plumbing the depths
    for a sin-ruined heart
indifferent to Thee;
    draining the dregs
of God's holy wrath
    that I might go free.

I looked into your face and knew
    that you were true;
those clear, deep eyes awoke in me
    a trust in you.

I'd dreamt of shoulders broad and straight,
    one built to lead;
I met you once and knew that you
    were all I need.

You did not have to say a word
    to make me feel
that will, completely in control,
    was made of steel.

I'd dreamt of dashing love and bold,
    life wild with zest;
but when with you my heart was stilled
    to perfect rest.

And how? I could not understand,
    it seemed so odd:
till on my heart it quietly dawned
    —love is of God!

As the portrait is unconscious
of the master artist's touch,
unaware of growing beauty,
unaware of changing much,
so you have not guessed His working
in your life throughout each year,
have not seen the growing beauty
have not sensed it, Mother dear.
We have seen and marveled greatly
at the Master Artist's skill,
marveled at the lovely picture
daily growing lovelier still;
watched His brush strokes
change each feature
to a likeness of His face,
till in you we see the Master,
feel His presence, glimpse His grace;
pray the fragrance of His presence
may through you seem doubly sweet,
till your years on earth are ended
and the portrait is complete.

It won't be long—
the sun is slowly slipping out of sight;
lengthening shadows deepen into dusk;
still winds whisper;
all is quiet:
it won't be long
—till night.

It won't be long—
the tired eyes close,
her strength is nearly gone;
frail hands that ministered to many
lie quiet, still;
Light from another world!
Look up, bereaved!
It won't be long
—till Dawn!

College and Early Love Poems

You held my hand
and I,
feeling a strange,
sweet thrill,
gave to my heart
a sharp rebuke,
and told it
to be still.

You held me close
and I
gasped, "Oh, no!"
until
I felt my heart within me rise
and tell me
to be still.

Train our love
that it may grow
slowly . . . deeply . . . steadily;
till our hearts will overflow
unrestrained and readily.

Discipline it, too,
dear God;
strength of steel
throughout the whole.
Teach us patience,
thoughtfulness,
tenderness, and
self-control.

Deepen it
throughout the years,
age and mellow it
until, time that finds us
old without,
within,
will find us
lovers still.

Dear God, I prayed, all unafraid
(as we're inclined to do),
I do not need a handsome man
but let him be like You;
I do not need one big and strong
nor yet so very tall,
nor need he be some genius,
or wealthy, Lord, at all;
but let his head be high, dear God,
and let his eye be clear,
his shoulders straight, whate'er his state,
whate'er his earthly sphere;
and let his face have character,
a ruggedness of soul,
and let his whole life show, dear God,
a singleness of goal;
then when he comes
(as he will come)
with quiet eyes aglow,
I'll understand that he's the man
I prayed for long ago.

God, make me worthy to be his wife:
as cliffs are made, so make me strong,
a help for him when things go wrong.
Clear as the dew, Lord, make my mind,
clear as the dew, and just as kind;
and let me be refreshing too,
—and quiet to remind you
with him to laugh in face of tears,
in face of worries and of fears;
brave to be and do and bear,
quick to yield and glad to share.
Let him know through coming days
my love is warm for him always.
His head's held high as he faces life;
God, make me worthy to be his wife.

It was so very good of God
  to let my dreams come true,
  to note a young girl's cherished hopes,
  then lead her right to you;
  so good of Him to take such care
  in little, detailed parts
  (He knows how much details mean
  to young and wishful hearts);
  so good of Him to let you be
  tall and slender, too,
  with waving hair more blond than brown
  and eyes of steel blue.

Lord, let mine be
a common place
while here.
His was a common one;
He seems so near
when I am working
at some ordinary task.
Lord, let mine be
a common one, I ask.
Give me the things to do
that others shun,
I am not gifted or so poised,
Lord, as some.
I am best fitted
for the common things,
and I am happy so.
It always brings
a sense of fellowship
with Him Who learned
to do the lowly things
that others spurned:

to wear the simple clothes,
the common dress,
to gather in His arms
and gently bless
(and He was busy, too)
a little child,
to lay his hand upon
the one defiled,
to walk with sinners
down some narrow street,
to kneel Himself
and wash men's dusty feet.
To ride a common foal,
to work with wood,
to dwell with common folk,
eat common food;
and then upon the city dump
to die for me

Lord, common things
are all I ask
of Thee.

An ancient oak
among the trees
stood in the freezing
Winter air;
lifeless it was
and stripped of leaves
only a few dead leaves
hung there.
I watched all Winter
—watched to see
how long
those shriveled leaves
would cling,
like withered hands,
upon the tree
where whipping winds
would bite and sting.
Each day I watched
and watched in vain;

snowstorms came
and blizzards blew,
wind, ice and sleet,
hailstorms and rain:
each took its turn.
When all was through,
those leaves
were still there
clinging fast.

Then—
came Spring.
Life throbbed anew
within the tree
and loosed their clasp.

*Y*our eyes
look down at me
so thoughtfully . . .
What do they see?
The plainness of me—
plainly built,
not small,
nor calmly poised,
nor quaint,
and, worst of all,
a nose upturned
and hands
that I have known
for years to be
too long,
too overgrown;
plain hazel eyes,
a face too pale,
not fair,
a mouth too large
and ordinary hair?
And all of me
tucked in
this homemade dress;
oh, if you look at me
so thoughtfully,
will you love me
the less?

I shall leave it here
beneath this star
tonight;
no one will see me
leave it
with only a star
for light;
no one will know
I stood here,
hoarding a heaviness,
clutching tightly
in eager hands
something of loveliness;
something
that struggled against me
striving for liberty:
I'll love it,
and leave it,
and then forget;
and forgetting—
I shall be free!

$\mathscr{D}$ear God,
let me soar in the face of the wind;
up—
up—
like the lark,
so poised and so sure,
through the cold
on the storm
with wings to endure.
Let the silver rain wash
all the dust from my wings,
let me soar
as he soars,
let me sing
as he sings;
let it lift me
all joyous
and carefree
and swift,
let it buffet
and drive me
but, God,
let it lift!

*D*ear one,
I was cross last night
and you had worked
so hard all day.
Quietly you said, "Good night,"
closed the door,
and went away.

Nights can be
so very long
when hearts are far
that should be near;
I cannot wait
for day to come
and hear you say
"Good morning,
Dear."

ray
     when all your soul
     on tiptoe stands
     in wistful eagerness
     to talk with God;
     put out your hands,
     God bends to hear;
     it would be sin
     not to draw near.
Pray
     when gray inertia
     creeps through your soul,
     as through a man
     who fights the cold,
     then growing languid
     slumbereth,
     and slumbering
     knows not
     it is death.
Pray
     when swamped
     with sin and shame
     and nowhere else
     to pin the blame
     but your own will
     and waywardness;
     God knows you,
     loves you nonetheless.
So . . . pray.

$\mathcal{T}$ell me
how
the setting sun,
briefly glimpsed
through wet
black clouds,
can
to molten gold
with ease,
kindle
sodden limbs
of trees.

*M*y love has long been yours . . .
since on that day
when we first met—
I will never quite forget
how you just paused
and smiled a bit,
then calmly helped yourself to it.

God,
let me be all he ever dreamed
of loveliness and laughter.
Veil his eyes a bit
because
there are so many little flaws;
somehow, God,
please let him see
only the bride I long to be,
remembering ever after—
I was all he ever dreamed
of loveliness and laughter.

Marriage
and Motherhood

With this ring . . ."
your strong, familiar voice
fell like a benediction
on my heart, that dusk;
tall candles flickered gently,
our age-old vows were said,
and I could hear
someone begin to sing
an old, old song,
timeworn and lovely,
timeworn and dear.
And in that dusk
were old, old friends—
and you,
an old friend, too,
(and dearer than them all).
Only my ring seemed new—
its plain gold surface
warm and bright
and strange to me
that candlelight . . .
unworn—unmarred
Could it be that wedding rings
like other things,
are lovelier when scarred?

$\mathcal{N}$ever let it end, God,
never—please—
all this growing loveliness,
all of these
brief moments of
fresh pleasure—
never let it end.
Let us always
be a little breathless
at love's beauty;
never let us
pause to reason
from a sense of duty;
never let us
stop to measure
just how much to give;
never let us
stoop to weigh love;
let us live—
and live!
Please, God,
let our hearts kneel always,
Love their only master,
knowing the warm impulsiveness
of shattered alabaster:
I know You can see things
the way a new bride sees,
so
never let it end, God,
never—please.

$\mathscr{D}$ear Lord,
    we've built this little house
    with sloping eaves, and windows wide,
    gray stone walls, and rustic doors,
    and paneled all inside.

We've prayed
    and planned and built this house.
    And here we pause, for You alone
    can by Your presence hallow it
    and make this house a home.

The field that night
was a sea of mud,
the wet sky
seared with flame;
each bursting shell,
like a blast from hell,
lit the spot
where a soldier fell.

There in the blackness,
lying low,
weakly
he spoke His name.

For
where the lust of man
runs loose
through stench and smoke
of hate white-hot,
where lives
and souls
are cheaply priced,
there walks the Christ.
The sin-scarred
brush
His white, white robes;
the wounded
touch His feet;

the dying whisper
His name in prayer,
wondering sweetly
to find Him there,
where hell
and the sinner meet.

~

He took of His grace . . .
His infinite grace . . .
And soldiers wondered
to find a trace
of tears
in the grime
on a dead man's face.
"The going
must've been tough,"
they said,
not knowing,
that death,
for a man
forgiven by God,
is easy going.

$\mathcal{I}$'m Daniel Creasman's mother.
I brung these clothes
so's you
could dress him up real natural-like—
no . . .
navy wouldn't do.
He liked this little playsuit—
it's sorta faded now—
that tore place he
he got tryin'
to help his daddy plow.
No . . .
if he dressed real smart-like—
and all that fancy trim—
the last we'd see of Danny,
it wouldn't seem
like him.
But . . .
comb his hair . . . real special . . .
(if 'twouldn't seem
too odd) . . .
I brush it so
come Sunday
when he goes
to the house of God."

That afternoon
I saw him—
so still, so tanned he lay—
with the faded blue suit on him,
like he'd just come in from play . . .
but his hair was brushed
"real special" . . .
and it didn't seem
one bit odd, for . . .
he was just a small boy,
done with play
gone home to the house of God.

*B*less him,
Lord,
in leaving
all
for You—
bereft;
bless him,
Lord,
put pity
the left.

Bless the sacrificial,
yielding
the dearly priced;
bless him,
Lord,
but pity
the sacrificed.

Bless each valiant warrior
wherever he
may roam;
bless him,
Lord;
but pity
those back home.

Ours is a little home
newly begun.
So, we would ask of Thee,
Lord, let it always be
chuck full of fun.

Homes, even newest ones,
often are full of
things unexpected, gray;
so let it be alway
bursting with love.

This, and above it all,
one special plea:
'mid outward storms, still it
and storm or calm, fill it,
Lord, full of Thee.

Miscellaneous

*L*ike Pharisees
do we condemn
before both man and God,
one who slipped
and whose clothing
is smeared with sod;

Could we but hear
His voice,
stern above our own,
"let him without sin
among you,
cast the first stone."

Abraham,
the friend of God,
with an only son
and a knife at his belt,
". . . Hero of faith."
Yet I've wondered
at times
how Isaac felt:
his father's hand
stretched forth to kill,
—himself the sacrificial lamb . . .
It does not say:
yet he grew
to serve
the God of his father
Abraham.

$\mathcal{I}$s the tree that's pruned
preoccupied with pain?
—standing with its wound
in the wind and rain;
shrouded in cool mist,
kissed by the dew,
chosen for a nest
by a bird or two;
enveloped by fragrance
of rainwashed air,
bloodroots and violets
clustered round it there;
gently transfigured
as sap begins to flow—
leaves, flowers,
choicest fruit—
how I'd like to know:
Is the tree that's pruned
preoccupied with pain?

I met you years ago
when
of all the men
I knew,
you,
I hero-worshiped
then:
you are my husband now,
my husband!
and from my home
(your arms),
I turn to look
down the long trail of years
to where I met you first
and hero-worshiped,
and I would smile;
. . . I know you better now:
the faults,
the odd preferments,
the differences
that make you you.
That other me
—so young,
so far away—
saw you
and hero-worshiped
but never knew;
while I,
grown wiser
with the closeness of these years,
hero-worship, too!

I am thy shield,
and thy
exceeding great reward."
Could heart wish more
than this,
O Lord,
my Lord?

The candle flames
of poplars,
in the little coves
burn low;
the woods, leaf-carpeted
are warm
with Autumn's afterglow.
There's frost
upon the air tonight,
a hint of coming cold;
still, the warmth
of Summer lingers
in the crimson
and the gold.

Give me a cove
—a little cove—
when Fall comes
amblin' round:
hint of frost
upon the air,
sunlight
on the ground;
a little cove
with poplars—

calm
and
straight
and
tall;
to burn like candle flames
against
the sullen gray
of Fall.

P. S.
We bought this cove
when coves were cheap,
flatland scarce,
mountains steep.
Not once
were we ever told
in Autumn
poplars
turn to gold.

Oh, it was cheap
(beyond belief)
but Autumn makes me feel
a thief.

*T*his is My body
broken like bread for you;
this is My blood
like water shed for you."
Drink it—and wonder.
Marvel—and eat.
God torn asunder,
man made complete!
Stagger the mind
at Truth here revealed:
kneel—and be broken,
rise—and be healed.
Go out and die,
die, 'live, and live!
Take all He offers,
take all and give.
Here's a remembering
to scorch and to bless:
sinners partaking
God's righteousness.

Lord, this is my body . . .

The day is long
and all that I must do
too much for my small strength.
When at length
the day is through,
shall I find
I failed to tap
the Infinite Resources
forever open to the weak
who seek?
Shall I die
regretting
not getting?
Shall Joy
weep
for my sake
—who would not
take?

*W*hat of the folk back home
that day
the sudden storm swept Galilee?
Knowing the violence of those storms,
the smallness of the craft,
did they
abandon themselves to grief,
or say,
"The One who sails with them
is He
Who made the storm-filled universe,
the height,
the depth,
the everywhere;
the storm is fierce,
the craft is small,
but
He is there!"?

*F*ive I have:
each separate,
distinct,
a soul
bound for eternity:
and I
—blind leader of the blind—
groping and fumbling,
casual and concerned,
by turns . . .
undisciplined, I seek
by order and command
to discipline and shape;
(I who need Thy discipline
to shape
my own disordered soul).
O Thou
Who seest the heart's
true, deep desire,
each shortcoming and
each sad mistake,
supplement
and
overrule,
nor let our children be
the victims of our own
unlikeness unto Thee.

Samson—
man of giant strength—
pillowed his great head upon
the lap of sin
then rose at length
"not knowing
that his strength was gone."

*D*ie, son:
but do not sin.
It is too high a price
for living—
if "life" it can be called
to wallow
(briefly even)
in that which God forbids.
Satan has desired you:
shrewd,
he will not use
revolting sins
to lure,
but "lovely" ones,
"respectable,"
"desirable,"
and "pure"
(or so they seem);

far better you should die
honorably,
and clean
than craven-hearted,
nearsighted,
weak of will
and mean,
your birthright you should sell
for a mere mess of pottage,
squander your inheritance
in wild living,
then fain
fill your belly with
the husks of swine.

Would you trade
fellowship with Him
for tarnished coin
and raveled end of rope?

God's hand is on you, son;
far better then
the furnace, seven-times heated,
the denned and starving lions,
the stones that honored Stephen,
or a cross . . .

The choice is yours:
God grant you
eyes to see
and ears to hear,
a loyal heart
and will of steel,
forged to His will,
sound in His fear.

So . . .
die;
but do not sin;

such death
is not life's end—
but its beginning.

It seems but yesterday
you lay
new in my arms.
Into our lives you brought
sunshine
and laughter—
play—
showers, too,
and song.
Headstrong,
heartstrong,
gay,
tender beyond believing,
simple in faith,
clear-eyed,
shy, eager for life—
you left us
rich in memories,
little wife.
And now today
I hear you say
words wise beyond your years;
I watch you play
with your small son,
tenderest of mothers.
Years slip away—

today
we are mothers
together.

The little things that bug me,
resentments deep within;
the things I ought to do, undone,
the irritations one by one
till nerves stretch screaming-thin
and bare for all the world to see—
which needs His touch to make it whole
the most, my body or my soul?

I pray—but nothing comes out right,
my thoughts go flying everywhere;
my attitudes are all confused,
I hate myself—I am not used
to hands all clenched, not clasped, in prayer,
and heart too leaden to take flight;
which, oh, which, needs to be whole
the most, my body or my soul?

I cannot read. I cannot pray.
I cannot even think.
Where to from here? and how get there
with only darkness everywhere?
I ought to rise and only sink . . .
and feel His arms, and hear Him say,
"I love you." . . . It was all my soul
or body needed to be whole.

All my leaves have fallen,
and all the world can see
where I hid my little nest
safe, within this tree.

All my leaves have fallen,
and yet, another year,
when I have need to hide my nest,
the leaves will reappear.

Carefree, she ran into the park to play,
her face uplifted to the sun
that day . . .
While I
aware of brewing storms
that eched
the sky,
clutched at a fear
and nursed it.
Then I
saw her hand
outstretched
like a small child;
and while I watched,
Another Hand
reached down and clasped it.

I heard the distant thunder
with a smile.

"The Lord said that he would dwell in the thick darkness."

1 Kings 8:12 KJV

"When I said, darkness will surely trample me down, then to my great joy, night was luminous."

Psalm 138:11, LXX, Septuagint

The growing darkness closes in
like some thick fog,
engulfing me—
a creeping horror—
till I learned,
"the darkness hideth not
from Thee."

"The earth was without form
and void."
Upon the deep
such darkness lay:
O Light, Who first created light,
do Thou the same
today!

As in a darkened room
one knows—
knows without sight—
another there,
so, in the darkness,
sure I knew
Thy presence,
and the cold despair,
formless and chaotic, merged
to a soft glory;
as a child
terrified by dark,
lies quiet
within his mother's arms,
no wild
fears shall torment,
my weakness now.
The dark—the dark—
surrounds me still.
But so cost Thou!

For all these smallnesses
I thank You, Lord:

small children
and small needs;
small meals to cook,
small talk to heed,
and a small book
from which to read
small stories;
small hurts to heal,
small disappointments, too,
as real
as ours;
small glories
to discover
in bugs,
pebbles,
flowers.

When day is through
my mind is small,
my strength is gone;
and as I gather
each dear one
I pray, "Bless each
for Jesus' sake—
such angels sleeping,
imps awake!"
What wears me out
are little things:
angels minus
shining wings.
Forgive me, Lord,
if I have whined—
it takes so much
to keep them shined;
yet each small rub
has its reward,
for they have blessed *me*.

Thank you,
Lord.

I knew a Malchus once.
Severely wounded
by a Peter's sword:
crazed by anger,
dazed by pain,
he thrust aside
with awful pride
that Gentle Hand
Whose touch alone
could make him
whole again.
"Have Jesus touch me?
Hell!" he hissed,
" 'twas His disciple
swung the sword,
aiming for my neck
and missed;
I want no part
of Peter's Lord!"

Strong Savior Christ
so oft repelled,
for rash disciples
blamed!

Poor wounded fools,
by pride compelled
to go on living
—maimed.

*L*ove
without clinging;
cry
if you must—
but privately cry;
the heart will adjust
to the newness of loving
in practical ways:
cleaning
and cooking
and sorting out clothes,
all say, "I love you,"
when lovingly done.

So—
love
without clinging;
cry—
if you must—
but privately cry;
the heart will adjust
to the length of his stride,
the song he is singing,
the trail he must ride,
the tensions that make him
the man that he is,
the world he must face,
the life that is his.

So
love
without clinging;
cry—
if you must—
but privately cry;
the heart will adjust
to being the heart,
not the forefront of life;
a part of himself,
not the object—
his wife.

So—
love!

When my Fall comes
I wonder
Will I feel
as I feel now?
glutted with happy memories,
content
to let them lie
like nuts
stored up against the coming cold?
Squirrels always gather
so I'm told
more than they will ever need;
and so have I.

Will the dry,
bitter smell of Fall,
the glory of the
dying leaves,
the last brave rose
against the wall,
fill me with quiet ecstasy
as they do now?

Will my thoughts turn
without regret,
to the warm comforts
Winter brings
of hearth fires,
books,
and inner things
and find them nicer yet?

$\mathcal{P}$uppet,
poor puppet,
who's pulling your strings?

Puppets can't answer,
puppets just swing;
puppets just hang there
docile and sweet,
kill on command
and riot in the street.

Puppet,
poor puppet,
who's pulling your strings?

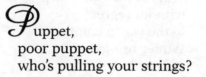

Over on Little Piney Ridge,
half a mile from my window sill,
the trees, stripped down
to their Winter briefs,
crowded together along the hill
as if for warmth,
and all was still;
when one small,
stubborn,
wrinkled,
leaf,
caught by a stray breeze
passing by,
sprang to life,
waved,
and caught my eye—
Over on Little Piney Ridge.

$\mathcal{I}$ cannot look You in the face,
God—
these eyes—
bloodshot,
bleary,
blurred;
shoulders slumped,
soul slumped,
heart too blank to care;
fears
worn out by fearing,
life
worn bare by living;
—living?
too old to live,
too young to die.
Who am I?
God—
Why?

They met
as two boats meet:
one headed into the Harbor,
one for the open sea.
And we wonder
which
will follow
which.

Never turn your back
on tears,
do not stem the flow;
put your arms about her
gently,
let her go.

Knowing why
is not important,
weeping
sometimes is.
Let her cry
—but kindly—
with a kiss.

In the weary,
waiting,
silence
of the night,
speak to me, Lord!
The others do—
haunting,
accusing,
foreboding;
the body tosses
and the heart grows tight,
and sleep,
elusive, fades into
the
weary,
waiting,
silence
of the night.

He speaks:
the mind,
preoccupied with
sleeplessness,
is deaf.
Silently
He wraps me in His love;
so loved,
I rest.

*P*lenty
is always provision for a need:
another's
or some future of our own—
unrealized, perhaps;
unseen.
The seven years of plenty
Joseph stored
against the years of famine
that would come.
So
when a winter
promises to be
severe,
nature generously provides
for little friends;
and sensing
in her lavish spread
a hint of coming want,
the ants
and squirrels are busy
harvesting;

and so am I.
I have been
so generously provided for
in happiness,
good memories,
family,
and true friends;
and more than all—
His presence and His Word;
perhaps it is a "sign,"
as mountain people say,
that winter is to be
a tough one.
If that is so,
let it be;
my larders are well stocked.

*D*eath—
death can be faced,
dealt with,
adjusted to,
outlived.
It's the
not knowing
that destroys
interminably . . .
This
being suspended
in suspense;
waiting—weightless.
How does one face
the faceless,
adjust to nothing?
Waiting implies
something to wait for.
Is there?

There is One.
One Who knows
where he is
and if;
and if he is,
is with him;
and if not,
is with me.
God, Thou art!
I rest my soul on that.

I rest him,
my hopes,
my fears,
my all—
on That.
Someday
I shall know,
and knowing
worship.
So—
today
I worship, too.

*T*urbulent ocean
billowing clouds
numinous
reflecting
briefly glorified
by the westering sun
incandescent
washed reflection
in the surf
easing out . . .
Wind in my face
and the waves sighing
moment of glory,
soul-catching,
gone.

Gulls
and sandpipers
looking for food.

*T*heirs
is a still-less,
restless grave—
dismantled
by each churning wave,
each tugging tide,
and pried
by treasure seekers, till
they know no rest
—who should be still.

One offered me
old coin for new;
priced as high
as they were few;
I held them in my hands
with awe—
two hundred years
I touched and saw,
but thought,
treasure should be found—
not bought.

And so, I searched:
training my eyes
to spot time's clever,
sure disguise.
My mind wheeled freely
with the gulls,
watching for cannon,
rusting hulls,
probing for treasure
(beneath that vast
impersonal guardian
of the past—
slapping indifferently
the beach),
buried,
barnacled,
out of reach.

A wistful beggar
asked an alm
from that
vast,
wet,
unyielding palm.

Then . . .

I thought of old,
wrecked lives
yielding
their treasure store
with each new storm;
and I had found,
not what I sought,
but more.

I will lift up mine eyes
to the hills";
and when I fly
I will lift up my eyes
instead
to the sky;
it is the same
sure,
certain thing—
this quiet lifting up,
remembering . . .

I leave myself
awhile
to let my thoughts
explore
all He has made
and more;
returning
to my small load
at length,
calm,
reassured:
this
is my strength.

The load
that lay
like lead
lifted;
instead:
peace.
The dread
that hung
fogthick, gray,
faded away;
and with release,
day.
The trial
the same . . .
unsolved,
but this:
now
it is
His.

*T*hat was the Day Between
the Night Before—

The blood
still wet upon the hill;
His body
wrapped,
entombed,
and still;
the great stone sealed
with Roman seal
and guarded well.

Many a Judean home
had now become
a lesser tomb
within whose walls
men lay,
whose Life had died
That Day.

Looking back
we cannot share
their black
despair.
For us
He is the Risen Christ,
as He had said:
for them, that Shabbat,
all life died—
for He was dead.

That was the Day Between
the Night Before.

This is my Day Between
my Night Before . . .

Suspended
in this interim—
let me be still,
let me adore,
let me remember
Him.

It seems irreverent
to fly above
snowcapped peaks;
mountains high enough
to earn the snows,
deserve respect;
they were made
to be looked up to,
not down upon,
by man.

～

Fly humbly,
when you fly;
walk,
when you can.

O tenderest Love,
how we do fail
through our own folly
to avail
ourselves of You.
Cold,
we shun
Your warmth,
Your sun;
dry,
Your dew,
Your everflowing Spring;
and pressured much,
we miss Your gentle,
calming touch;
then wonder, "Why?"
O pitying Heart,
forgive
the pauper spirit
that would live
a beggar
at Your Open Gate
until it is too late
—too late.

*P*erhaps
she will land
upon That Shore,
not in full sail,
but rather,
a bit of broken wreckage
for Him
to gather.

Perhaps
He walks Those Shores
seeking such,
who have believed
a little,
suffered much
and so,
been washed Ashore.

Perhaps
of all the souls redeemed
they most
adore.

*H*e is not eloquent
as men count such;
for him
words trip and stumble
giving speech
an awkward touch,
and humble:
so, much
is left unsaid
that he would say
if he were eloquent.
Wisely discontent,
compassion driven
(as avarice drives some,
ambition others),
the old,
the lonely,
and the outcast come;
all are welcome,
all find a home,
all—his brothers.
Behind him
deeds rise quietly
to stay;
and those with eyes to see
can see
all he can say.

Perhaps he'd not have spent
his life this way
if he were eloquent.

This is my ledge
of quiet,
my shelf of peace,
edged
by its crooked rails
holding back the beyond.
Above,
a hawk sails
high
to challenge clouds
trespassing
my plot of sky.
Below
in the valley,
remote and dim,
sounds
come and go,
a requiem
for quiet.
Here on my ledge,
quiet praise:
of birds,
crickets,
breeze—
in different ways;
and so do I—
for these:
my ledge of quiet,
my plot of sky:
for peace.

$\mathcal{N}$ot fears
I need deliverance from
today—
but nothingness;
inertia,
skies gray
and windless;
no sun,
no rain,
no stab of joy
or pain,
no strong regret,
no reaching after,
no tears,
no laughter,
no black despair,
no bliss.
Deliver me
today
. . . from this.

An owl hooted mournfully this noon:
incongruous, if you please,
as Jeremiah prophesying doom
in midst of peace.

He hung his heart
on a fence for sale,
then sat in his van
and watched them pass:
some, just out for a Sunday stroll,
glancing at the art *en masse;*
others, curious; and a few,
souvenir hunting
(as tourists do)
paused to price as well as stare;
—and part of himself
hung drying there:
years of feeling,
hours of toil—
(acrylic was faster;
he chose oil).
So when some tourist asked,
"How much?"
He'd smile and say,
"It's wet. Don't touch."
He needed to sell his work
and yet . . .

*W*hen a young boy cries
in bed at night,
stealthily, silently,
never aloud,
newly away
from family and friends,
too old to cry,
too proud;
too young to know
each night passes on
making way
for a newer dawn;
too old
to stay
in the nest, and yet
too young
to fly
away.
God,
be near
when a young boy cries.

I walked today
through loud, crisp leaves;
back to the sun,
face to the breeze;
and where I sat
to enjoy the view,
a grasshopper sat
enjoying it, too:
("of sober color,"
except for thighs,
protectively striped,
which did seem wise).
And there in the warm sun,
side by side,
each viewed the view
and each one eyed
the other. Odd, we two:
below us lay
the valley floor
which Fall, with blue haze,
failed to smother;
splendor unmatched
on which to gaze—
and each
distracted by the other!

I love these last details of Fall
when past its prime;
the graying hills,
no longer color-crowded, climb,
subdued, to meet a brilliant sky;
when sunlight spills,
filtering through branches
newly bare,
to warm
a newly covered ground,
and light the way
for tired leaves
still falling down.
To see a spray of yellow leaves
illumining wet,
rain-blackened trees,
stabs with a joy
akin to pain
that pauses
but to stab again:

when round the corner,
like a shout,
a single, crimson
tree stands out!
After the whole is bedded down
upon the earth's
vast compost heap,
and sight gives place
to faith and hope,
walking up the mountain slope,
lying on my path I find
a last bright leaf
for me to keep.

Beauty distilled
by solitude,
unrivaled by
the burned out wood;
glory unfurled
against a world
stripped and chilled—
by death subdued;
such lonely,
gay defiance speaks
more than Fall's prime
could,
more than Fall's peak.

*I*f I could have each day
one hour of sun,
glorious,
healing,
hot,
like now—
then
let Winter come!
Not
mild and brief,
but
wild, without relief;
let the storms rage,
let the winds blow,
the freezing rains
lashing my windowpanes;
then
let it snow!
long
and
deep
and cold.
I would not mind at all:
it would be fun . . .
if I could have
each day
my hour of sun.

Show me a small
and shriveled seed,
discarded
as a worthless thing:
smile
if you will,
that I should kneel
in worship
—there'll be Spring!

There will be less someday—
much less,
and there will be More:
less to distract
and amuse;
More, to adore;
less to burden
and confuse;
More, to undo
the cluttering of centuries,
that we might view
again, That which star
and angels
pointed to;
we shall be poorer—
and richer;
stripped—and free:
for always there will be a Gift,
always
a Tree!

*T*hose were no ordinary sheep . . .
no common flocks,
huddled in sleep
among the fields,
the layered rocks,
near Bethlehem
That Night;
but those
selected for the Temple sacrifice:
theirs to atone
for sins
they had not done.

〜

How right
the angels should appear
to them
That Night.

〜

Those were no usual shepherds
there,
but outcast shepherds
whose unusual care
of special sheep
made it impossible to keep
Rabbinic law,
which therefore banned them.

〜

How right
the angels should appear
to them
That Night.

Sitting by my laughing fire
I watch the whitening world without,
and hear the wind climb higher, higher,
rising to a savage shout;
and on my hearth
the logs smile on,
warming me
as they slowly perish;
they had been felled
by ax and saw
while fellow trees
were left to flourish;
but what was spared
by ax and saw,
by some unspoken,
cruel law,
was being harvested without
by ice and wind and savage shout.

∾

And on my hearth
the logs smile on.

$\mathcal{F}$or all
who knew the shelter of The Fold,
its warmth and safety
and The Shepherd's care,
and bolted;
choosing instead to fare
out into the cold,
the night;
revolted
by guardianship,
by Light;
lured
by the unknown;
eager to be out
and on their own;
freed
to water
where they may,
feed
where they can,
live as they will:
till
they are cured,
let them be cold,
ill;

let them know terror,
feed
them with thistle,
weed,
and thorn;
who chose
the company of wolves,
let them taste
the companionship wolves give
to helpless strays;
but, oh! let them live—
wiser, though torn!
And wherever,
however far away
they roam,
follow
and
watch
and
keep
Your stupid, wayward, stubborn sheep,
and someday
bring them Home!

I awoke heavy
and heavy I prayed,
face in the sun,
heart in the shade.
As smoke hangs low
on a sullen day,
my prayer hung there . . .
till I heard His voice,
"This is the day
that the Lord hath made";

Rejoice!

*L*ow gray skies,
clouds
moving fast,

crowds . . .
one man,
and a flag
half mast.

Of this historic moment
two things I kept:
that earth was gray
and cold,
and heaven wept.

*L*arger than life
he lived here,
smaller than death
he lies
under the spreading oak trees,
under the skies.

If mercy is for sinners,
(which God
in mercy gives)
smaller than Life
he lived here,
larger than death
he lives.

You look at me
and see
my flaws;
I look at you
and see flaws, too.
Those who love,
know love
deserves
a second glance;
each failure serves
another chance.
Love looks to see,
beyond the scars
and flaws,
the cause;
and scars become
an honorable badge
of battles fought
and won—
(or lost) but fought!
The product,
not the cost,
is what love sought.

~

God help us see
beyond the now
to the before,
and note with tenderness
what lies between
—and love the more!

Those seals—
weight of empires,
authority of kings;
dread power
compressed to make
it worth one's life
to break
those seals;
no mortal dared;
no matter when,
no matter whom.
One secured
a lion's den;
one
a borrowed tomb.

A burst of song
as the bird flew by,
hotly pursued
by an angry bird;
I saw,
I heard,
not knowing why,
or which was right
or wrong,
nor whence they came
nor went.
I only know
that burst of flight,
that mocking song,
is mine to keep
for merriment,
for long.

The hills were hunkered down in mist,
grizzled against the wetting sky;
I felt the earth's cold loneliness—
I saw her cry,
splattering my windows with her tears;
each little hollow held a cloud,
each had its share of separate grief,
each—its shroud.

O Thou,
Whose stillness drowns
earth's total noise—
its grating sounds:
progress,
traffic,
voice;
flutterings
of my frustration,
mutterings,
agitation;
the screaming silences
without,
within;
the din
of questions clamoring
for their "why?"
and "how?"
now!
the rumblings
of man's discontent,
erupting hate,
violence;

war's distant thunder
rolling near,
and everywhere
the cries
of fear
that paralyzes
as it grips . . .
and near at hand
a faucet drips.

O Thou,
Whose stillness drowns
earth's total noise,
only in Thee
is stillness found . . .
And I rejoice.

*W*inter speaks
to the surfeited heart,
weary of heat
and weeds
and leaves,
longing to breathe
cold, bracing air,
explore the hillsides
swept and bare;
to revel in each bush,
each tree
stripped to stark
simplicity;
original etchings
everywhere—
and You,
Who etched them,
with me there.

Atop the ridge
against the sky
where clouds,
windwhipped,
sail free, sail high,
a tree uprooted,
fell and lodged
in the forks of an oak tree
standing by.

There they stood—
felled,
upheld,
in the windswept wood.
Atop the ridge
I found them there
one cold Spring day;
and stopped
to stare;

and stayed
to pray.

It is this stillness
that I find oppressive:
after the wind
that blew across these hills,
howling around the house—
violent and possessive,
prowling the sills,
slamming the shutters
(if it found one loose),
dying to threatening mutters
and rising to shake
the ancient oak,
hoping some branch
would break—
and when it broke,
chasing the hapless leaves
into whatever corner
they could find
shelter in;

"Oh be kind!"
I'd think, watching it whip and tear
smoke from the chimney
like a thing alive,
whirling it to the ground;
then drive the clouds
as if they were a flock
of frightened sheep.
How long it blew—
a lifetime or a day—
I never knew;
it went away
somewhere near five o'clock,
leaving earth still and thinned:
and I could weep—
who had grown used
to wind.

$\mathcal{H}$ad I been Joseph's mother
I'd have prayed
protection from his brothers:
"God keep him safe;
he is so young,
so different from
the others."
Mercifully she never knew
there would be slavery
and prison, too.

Had I been Moses' mother
I'd have wept
to keep my little son;
praying she might forget
the babe drawn from the water
of the Nile,
had I not kept
him for her
nursing him the while?
Was he not mine
and she
but Pharaoh's daughter?

Had I been Daniel's mother
I should have pled
"Give victory!
This Babylonian horde—
godless and cruel—
don't let them take him captive
—better dead,
Almighty Lord!"

Had I been Mary—
Oh, had I been she,
I would have cried
as never a mother cried,
". . . Anything, O God,
anything . . .
but crucified!"

With such prayers
importunate
my finite wisdom
would assail
Infinite Wisdom;
God, how fortunate
Infinite Wisdom
should prevail!

Beyond those hills
lie yesterday,
the silenced now,
and a tomorrow.
The clouds
that wrap those hills
like shrouds
are free to come and go
at will:
no guns can frighten
them away
nor stop the moon
and stars, nor say
the sun must shine.
No manifesto tells the rain
where it must fall,
how much
and when.

The very air
they breathe
(on which their life depends)
comes from the One
Whom they deny.
And yet He sends
them rain and sun
and air to breathe.
And here and there
does one look up
and see,
and know He is,
and He is There?

*M*ay she have daughters
of her own to care
when she is old
and I am gone.
I should have loved
to care for her once more
as I did then
long years before.
I was a mother young
and she—my child.
Caring was joy. So when
she is old and I am There,
may she have daughters
of her own
to care.

Oh, time! be slow!
it was a dawn ago
I was a child
dreaming of being grown;
a noon ago
I was
with children of my own;
and now
it's afternoon
—and late—
and they are grown
and gone.
Time, wait!

The hills on which I need to gaze
are wrapped in clouds again.
I lift up streaming eyes in vain
and feel upon my upturned face
the streaming rain.

eath, be not long.
Death, be not hard."
But days stretched year-like
and when death came,
God,
it was not easy
as we had prayed.
Quiet, but not easy.

Forgive my complaints;
for precious to You
is the death of Your saints.

*M*anicured, styled,
expensively suited,
they stood
and they smiled
as if programmed, computed
by specialists fed;
yet I knew within each
beat a heart living-dead.
The smiles were a mask;
the lifestyles they led
at best a brave showing,
pretending, not being,
while You Who created
are God, the Allknowing,
are God, the Allseeing.

Lord, we cannot see
as You see above,
behind and within. We
only can love.

Odd
this twisted form
should be
the work of
God.

God
Who makes,
without mistakes,
the happy norm,
the status quo,
the usual,
made me,
you know.
The Royal Palm
He made;
and, too,
the stunted pine.
With joy
I see the lovely shapes.
With pride
I live in mine.

~

No accident I am:
a Master Craftsman's plan.

Do You not care, Lord?
Do You not see?
"What is that to thee?"
He said,
"Follow thou Me."

$\mathcal{G}$od,
what a waste!
He was so needed
by us all
. . . by You.
and yet You kill,
it seems at will,
Your young,
Your trained,
Your highly skilled
(and not a few)—
Stephen first
. . . then James . . .
and . . .
O God!
our Savior, too.
Did I say
"waste"?
Forgive
the stupid words
we cry
in anguished haste.
The Gardener
plants
and reaps
with skill.

. . . it's only
that we're left here
still.

When
in the morning
I make our bed,
pulling his sheets
and covers tight,
I know the tears
I shouldn't shed
will fall unbidden
as the rain;
and I would kneel,
praying again
words I mean
but cannot feel.

"Lord,
not my will
but Thine
be done."
The doubts dissolving
one by one . . .

For I will realize
as I pray,
that's why it happened
. . . and this way.

*T*onight
I have a roof of slate
to look upon.
Cool rain,
like Scottish mist,
falls gently and
the sun is gone
—setting late—
and I am still,
listening to
the reassuring of a dove
upon the sill;
a long day's journey
ending thus
in tired ease,
above a cobbled courtyard
grayed with age,
wrapped in peace. . . .

"The gates of Hell are locked
from the inside."

C. S. Lewis

*I*f that is so,
  he seemed already there;
  his guarded eyes
  looked out at me
  as if through bars;
  my words fell unheard
  on the stale air,
  my heart reached out
  and touched a closing door,
  the widening gulf between
  already wide.
  "I pray for you,"
  I said and said no more.
  The vacant eyes withdrew.

Was the key turning
on the other side?

*L*et it be twilight
just a little longer . . .
don't turn the lights up
yet;
twilight's a time
for remembering,
twilight's a time
to forget;
a decompression chamber
where the soul
submerged, uptight,
can un-begin
and slowly rise
to night.

And when I die
I hope my soul ascends
slowly, so that I
may watch the earth receding
out of sight,
its vastness growing smaller
as I rise,
savoring its recession
with delight.
Anticipating joy
is itself a joy.
And joy unspeakable
and full of glory
needs more
than "in the twinkling of an eye,"
more than "in a moment."

Lord, who am I to disagree?
It's only we
have much to leave behind;
so much . . . Before.
These moments
of transition
will, for me, be
time
to adore.

$\mathcal{H}$e took . . .
and blessed
and broke . . ."
the Scriptures say,
the bread
with which those hungry folk
were fed
that day.

And by this simple act
—so oddly His—
two, bewildered
by their loss
(whose Life had died
upon a cross,
pierced by nail and sword);
those two, eyes opened,
saw in this
their Risen Lord.

Lord,
when I dread
to be broken bread
and poured out wine
for You,
to satisfy man's hunger,
quench man's thirst,
remind me
how you blessed it
first.

$\mathcal{G}$od,
it grows darker
day by day;
blood stains the present
and the future may
well be history's dark night.
Deliverance (at times)
and yet death might
best serve Your ends.
You choose, not they
who do the deed.
They plot, You laugh.
You knew
when they had killed
before,
they did what You
had willed:
no less—
no more.

Lord, I am filled
with wonder
(who had been filled
with fears),
for
I hear Your laughter
when I hear the thunder,
and when I feel the raindrops,
feel Your tears.

I think it harder,
Lord, to cast
the cares of those I love
on You,
than to cast mine.
We, growing older,
learn at last
that You
are merciful
and kind.
Not one time
have You failed me,
Lord—
why fear that you'll fail mine?

*S*he waited for the call
that never came;
searched every mail
for a letter,
or a note,
or card,
that bore his name;
and on her knees
at night,
and on her feet
all day,
she stormed Heaven's Gate
in his behalf;
she pled for him
in Heaven's high court.

"Be still, and wait,"
the word He gave;
and so she knew
He would
do in, and for,
and with him,
that which she never could.
Doubts ignored,
she went about her chores
with joy;
knowing, though spurned,
His word was true.
The prodigal had not returned
but God was God,
and there was work to do.

God, look who my Daddy is!
He is the one
who wore his guardian angel out
(he thought it fun).
First, it was bikes:
he tore around those hills
like something wild,
breaking his bones
in one of many spills;
next, it was cars:
how fast he drove (though well)
only patrolmen
and his guardian angel knew
the first complained,
the second never tells.
Then it was planes:
that was the closest we
ever got—till now.
I never knew him well
except that he
kept that angelic guardian
on his toes.

Not long ago
You touched him,
and he turned.
Oh, Lord, what grace!
(And how quizzical the look
upon his angel's face:
a sort of skidding-to-a-stop
to change his pace.)
And now, he just had me:
which only shows
who needs a little angel of his own
to keep him on his toes.
Oh, humorous vengeance!
Recompense—with fun!
I'll keep him busy, Lord.
Well done! Well done!

To heal a hate
takes grace
that isn't. There
is churning hurt
and bitterness
—and black despair.
No love. No grace.
No power to choose.
I heard a stillness.
Then
I felt His face.
His searching eyes
held mine
and would not turn me loose.
Then through hot tears
I saw and understood:
He hung cross high,
a spear was in my hand
that dripped with blood,
a helmet on my head.

I watched Him die;
but just before, He said,
"Forgive them for
they know not what
they do" . . .
then He was dead.
Slowly I raise my head:
the clouds were unarranged,
the sky was fair,
the warm sun shone,
nothing had changed:
the hurt still there
only . . .
the hate was gone.

$\mathcal{I}$t was a lonely
desperate search
that led her up one street and down
another, looking for a church
where she could kneel and pray.
She looked Prague through
that somber day—
(what was left of a woman's heart
God knew).
Yet each was boarded up
(where does one take despair?),
on each a notice nailed:
"closed . . . for repair."

~

Year followed year:
wars . . .
elections . . .
death . . .
each country wrapped
within its own affairs.
The evening news
kept all aware
of Vietnam,
Ireland,
the Middle East,
and Chad.
Few ever thought of God's house
"closed . . . for repair,"
and if they had
nothing was said,
presuming it dead.
Till one day came
a writer without fear,
and those with time to read
took time to hear.
That which we thought was dead,
of which we all despaired,
showed signs of reemerging:
. . . repaired!

*W*e Peters walking
on life's sea,
implore ignoring grace
of heaving waves;
oh, let us be,
however weak,
intent on Thee;
our eyes upon Thy face.

$\mathcal{D}$on't crowd me.
I need room to grow,
to stretch my wings,
breathe deep and slow;
to look about,
to think things through;
don't hem me in,
don't block the view.
Don't push me;
I need time to grow,
to savor life from day
to day; freedom to go
at my own pace;
leisure to live more thoroughly,
unherded and unhurried, please;
just let me *BE*.
Don't stalk me.
Follow where He leads
though it may mean
another path, one needs
one single aim in life:
follow well, work hard,
obedient and faithful.
So go!—after God.

This is a gentle part of town
—run down.
Papers blow about the street,
people walk on tired feet,
discount stores, a place to eat,
hardware, garden stuff and such:
shabby. No, there isn't much
to see. And yet,
here's a part I can't forget.
It isn't something
I just feel:
but folks are folks here,
folks are real,
folks are simple,
folks are kind,
if you don't buy much
they don't mind.
It's just a gentle part of town
—run down.

$\mathcal{I}$t is no nightingale
tonight,
no whippoorwill,
enchanting pale
twilight
with singing
on the hill
for us . . .
only the limpid frogs,
hatched in the damp
someplace,
raising their hallelujah
chorus
loud . . .

and I am touched
with grace.

He does not go alone,
this gangling boy, all legs and arms;
awkward and gentle and so prone
to impulse judgment. What alarms
mothers at home, praying, sleepless, tense,
are all the "what ifs" Satan sends
as though in glee. And still I sense
he is accompanied, and apprehend
Divine forethought, guidance and, when needed,
an Intervening Hand. So I would pray
in wondering gratitude, for having heeded
God's promise, I can praise today.

A house
is not the same
when she
who made it home
is gone;
it looks
as it has always
looked
and yet
forlorn.
There is an emptines
within,
a silence
where her chuckle was.
From now on
it is me alone
who once was "us."

$\mathcal{A}$nd when Messiah comes,"
he said,
his eyes looked through me
and beyond,
the food forgotten
on his plate,
silent
he let the minutes wait
as light dawned,
"And when Messiah comes,"
he said,
the strange thought
gripped him
strong, sublime;
repelled and beckoned;
"I shall ask
is this the first time
. . . or the second?"

$\mathcal{I}$ captured him in Kleenex
and threw him out with care—
the happy little cricket
enlivening the air.
For it was late and I,
tired from the noise of day,
tossed sleepless, then decided my
rest precluded his play.
And so he was moved
without notice:
I didn't even wince;
But slept serenely all night long
. . . and have missed him
ever since.

$\mathcal{L}$eave it all quietly to God
my soul":
the past mistakes
that left
their scars.
All bitterness
beyond control,
that mars
His peace,
demands its toll.
Confessed to Him
. . . and left . . .
it would,
like all things
work together
for my good,
and bring release.
I would be whole.
So
"Leave it all quietly to God
my soul."

I need Your help
in the evening
more, I think,
than at dawn.
For tiredness comes
with twilight,
and my resolves are gone.
I'm thinking of rest
not service,
of valleys
instead of steeps,
and my dreams are not
of conquest
but the blissful oblivion
of sleep.

$\mathcal{W}$here does one turn
at such a time
as this?
Where find concern
that once was mine,
such bliss
as a loved child
knows within his home
when small?
The whole world smiled
and that loved home
was all.
Where does one turn
at such a time
as this?
Lord, but to You
Whose gentle "Come"
is assurance strong of love
of warmth and safety, too,
of bliss—
and I am Home.

We live a time
secure;
beloved and loving,
sure
it cannot last
for long
then—
the good-byes come
again—again—
like a small death,
the closing of a door.
One learns to live
with pain.
One looks ahead,
not back—
never back,
only before.
And joy will come again—
warm and secure,
if only for the now,
laughing,
we endure.

They felt good eyes upon them
and shrunk within—undone;
good parents had good children
and they—a wandering one.

The good folk never meant
to act smug or condemn,
but having prodigals
just "wasn't done" with them.

Remind them gently, Lord,
how You
have trouble with Your children,
too.

*W*e are told
to wait on You.
But, Lord, there is no time.
My heart implores upon its knees,
"Hurry! . . . please."

$\mathcal{M}$ay he face life's problems
as he faced
his broken bike
when he was small,
working till he'd traced
each problem to its source,
and fixed it; all
was a challenge he'd accept
with curiosity and then
work night and day.
What's losing sleep when
interest is involved?
Hobby or problem
he never turned it loose
till it was solved.
Now
he's a man.
And man-sized problems
stare him in the face.
Interested or not,
Lord,
give him grace.
As this is a problem tough,
and not a toy,
so, too, he is a man now,
Lord
—not a boy.

*(Yet in the boy he once was I could see
delightful glimpses of the man that he would be.)*

He handed it to me
then stood
shyly;
his face,
alight with pride,
searched mine to see
if I'd
be pleased or
if I would
note the flaws
which, even with my help,
were there
(obvious but understood)
because his heart was in the work
that he had done
(which my heart took);
he'd given me
the very best he could.

~

Lord—
here is my son.

How can I pray while my heart cries,
"You killed
my son"?
What can I say?
How look for comfort
from the One
Who willed
it done?
Omnipotent, He could
have stopped it
if He would;
my son . . . my son . . .
numb with grief,
my soul is one vast "why?"
his life was all too brief;
he was so young
to die.
Where were You,
Lord?
Where were You?
Gently He replied,
"Just where I was,
dearly, dearly loved,
when Mine
was crucified."

Don't talk to me yet;
the wound is fresh,
the nauseous pain
I can't forget
fades into numbness
like a wave,
then comes again.
Your tears I understand,
but grief is deaf;
it cannot hear the words
you gently planned
and tried to say.
But . . .
pray.

*T*hey say
I must not care so much,
or feel so deeply.
I shouldn't study
or read depressing books
like *Under the Rubble,*
or *China Today.*
Rather, I should play,
read Agatha Christie,
and relax.
Which would mean
bottling up my
deepest concerns,
turning off my mind,
and growing bored.
But heart and mind have
no faucets—"Hot" and "cold,"
no switch for
"on" and "off."
Cannot one live
with concern,
read deeply,
and still relax?
Concern, undergirded
with confidence,
knowing that God
is in control?

$\mathcal{I}$s there somewhere,
anywhere, . . .
a little, lonesome cabin
lost among the forests
on a wild, deserted shore;
an empty, waiting cabin:
rough-hewn, worn, and solid
with a dandy-drawing chimney,
books and windows little more
I'm tired of noise and traffic,
people pushing, phones and letters,
dates and deadlines, styles and headlines,
pride and pretense, nothing more;
and I'm needing such a cabin,
near God's masterpiece of mountains,
such a lost and lonesome cabin
where a tired soul can adore.

Beyond all custom
all tradition,
Lord, I would see
Your truth revealed;
then could I come,
in my condition,
to seek Your face,
and by Your grace
be healed.
What I confess
You long have known;
. . . acknowledge the gross mess
that my own sins have grown
like some wild
poisonous vine,
enmeshing other lives
with mine.
"Just as I am"
to me confirms
that none but You
would take one on such terms

For only You
Who went the length
of Calvary
could know
the cost
of such forgiving love,
redeeming strength,
or show
Satan and his hordes
justice has been done.

While I
defeated by that cross
freed from his cords,
kneeling,
glory in my loss
for You have won!

And for all
my sins have wounded
on the way
I plead Your special help:
for them I pray.

*S*harp eyes he had, you say?
Yet I'll wager
they were filled with tears
many a day.
His heart watched, too,
—for years;
and, busy as he was, he'd stand
filled with a yearning
for that son who'd left
for some far land,
spurning
love, and home—and him;
frantic for fun, debating
all he had learned;
and so, the Father stood
watching . . .
yearning . . .
waiting . . .
for his son's returning.

∿

Some would pity,
to see him grieve,
a few might scoff.
True,
the Father watched him leave
but, too,
He saw him coming
"when yet a great way off."

*W*hen we see
trying, guilty "saints"
(ourselves the guiltiest,
no doubt),
forgive us, Lord,
for our complaints;
and help us never
to forget,
whatever else, Lord,
You're about,
You have not finished
with us
—yet.

Theirs was a moment
of glory brief.
I watched them pass
in their long black gowns
before the graduation crowd
swiftly, silently
some with relief
to receive their diploma
(you couldn't mistake it,
they all but sighed,
as they reached to take it).
And when together
they sat back down,
the applause was long,
commanding, loud;
parents, relatives,
friends looked on
and each in his own way
was proud.
Then in the back,
quiet, withdrawn,
I glimpsed the one
who didn't make it.

*H*e sang atop the old split rail
all while it thundered,
raindrops pelting him like hail,
and, I wondered:

How one small, vulnerable bird,
defying deafening thunder,
could make itself so sweetly heard.
And still I wonder.

Enlarge my heart
to love You more,
when I am stumbling
on the way;
only the heart
enlarged by You
runs to obey.

*A*bove the clouds
thick, boiling, low,
appear the peaks
she came to know
as Father, Son,
and Holy Ghost.
Often when she
sought them most,
they would be hid,
in clouds, from view.

Distraught by cares,
she always knew,
silent, unseen,
they still were there
like God Himself—
unchanged, serene;
and knowing this,
she gathered strength
for each day's journey,
—length by length.

$\mathcal{S}$uch unorchestrated music
one has seldom heard:
dawn breeze
in the tops of trees
much liquid song of bird
sparrow,
robin,
towhee,
indigo bunting,
wren,
meadowlark
and cardinal,
mockingbird,
finch,
and when
my soul is on tiptoes,
filled with ecstasy,
the turkey gobbles loudly
down by the locust tree!

$\mathcal{I}$f
I could stand aside
and see
him walking through
those Splendor'd Gates
thrown wide,
instead of me—
If I could yield my place
to this, my boy,
the tears upon
my upturned face
would be
of joy!

I bring those whom I love
to You,
commit each to
Your loving care,
then carry them away again
nor leave them there:
forgetting You
Who lived to die
(and rose again!)
care more than I.

So back I come
with my heart's load
confessing
my lack of faith
in You alone,
addressing
all I cannot understand
to You,
Who do.

You know each heart,
each hidden wound,
each scar,
each one who played a part
in making those
we bring to You
the ones they are
(and dearer each to You
than us, by far).

So now I give them
to Your loving care,
with thankful heart,
and leave them there.

The Far Country
may be near,
beneath this roof
or down the street;
yet he is there,
and I am here,
and when we meet
there are those
lonesome miles between
that can be felt
but never seen.

*B*ut
what of the
ones
forsaken,
Lord,
—even for You?
The sons
now grown
who've never known
fathers who
had undertaken
to leave all
and follow You?
Some wounded beyond repair,
bitter, confused—lost—
these are the ones
for whom
mothers weep,
bringing to You
in prayer
nights they cannot sleep

—these,
Lord,
are what it cost.

$\mathcal{L}$ord,
in this frenzied puttering
around the house,
see more!
The dusting,
straightening,
muttering,
are but the poor
efforts of a heavy heart
to help time pass.
Praying on my knees
I get uptight;
for hearts and lives
are not the only things
that need to be
put right.

And, while I clean,
please,
if tears should fall,
they're settling the dust,
—that's all.
Lord, I will straighten
all I can
and You—
take over what we mothers
cannot do.

*L*ike other shepherds
help me keep
watch over my flock by night;
mindful of each need,
each hurt, which might
lead one to stray,
each weakness
and each ill—
while others sleep
teach me to pray.
At night the wolves and leopards,
hungry and clever, prowl
in search of strays,
and wounded; when they howl,
Lord, still
my anxious heart
to calm delight—
for the Great Shepherd
watches with me
over my flock
by night.

Another lamb
will join the fold
tonight:
Good Shepherd
welcome her,
we pray,
and hold
her tight.

God's gracious gifts
of sun and sea,
of gentle weather,
within reach
of each
whether
poor or rich.
Yet at times I wonder—
which is which?

There was only one
in the crowd that day,
with a smile
(instead of words) to say.
Standing there
with cane and brace,
the light of heaven
on her face.

We didn't say a lot
(there was no time
to share her story),
yet I had got
a touch of special grace,
a glimpse of glory.

God had her carry
quite a heavy cross
for Him awhile;
and she, aware of all it cost,
was answering
with a smile.

I am a primitive.
I love
primordial silences
that reign
unbroken over ridge
and plain,
unspoiled by
civilization's roar.
I love the lonesome sound
of wind,
the final crashing
of a tree,
the wash of waves
upon the shore,
wind, thunder, and
the pouring rain
are symphonies to me.

Jesus wept.
But why?
knowing what lay ahead
moments away . . .
Was it because
He had not come,
when He heard
Lazarus might die?
Lazarus was dead!
Was it in sympathy
with their raw grief,
faith's impotent lack?
Or could it be
because He
had to bring him
back?

❧

Leave a little light on
somewhere, in some room,
dark, rainy days;
where, in the deepening gloom,
I, damped and grayed
by weather, might
in some unexpected place
glimpse warmth and cheer.
Those who feel that light
is utilitarian only,
have never known
the desolation dusk can bring,
to being lonely.

They come and go so quickly
Spring and Fall . . .
as if they had not really
come at all.
Perhaps
we could not take
too much of beauty,
breath-catching glory,
ecstasy without relief;
and so
God made them
brief.

The unrelieved complaining
of the wind across the ridge,
rising of a sudden,
to a wild and lonesome roar,
like the sad, sustained resounding
of the surf upon some shore,
leaves my own heart strangely pounding
—as if I'd heard God sighing
for a world astray and dying,
and somewhere, a lost soul crying,
wanting more.

Be tender, Lord, we pray
with one whose child
lies dead today.

Be tenderer, Lord, we plead
for those with runaways
for whom Moms bleed.

But tenderest of all with each
whose child no longer cares
is out of reach.

*H*ave I been a wilderness to you?"
asked the Lord.
"A place of wandering
and of darkness
as the night?"

No . . .
It is this void
in which I find myself.
This is my wilderness,
my place of wandering
in darkness and in fog.
You are Light
and Life.
All I long for,
all I need,
is You.

How can we walk together
once again?
How can I know You, Lord,
as once I knew?

And He,
through the echoing of my empty heart
replied,
"I shall be waiting for you
at the very spot
you left my side."

Tonight
the lights went out
(aftermath of a sudden storm),
trapped in the dark
I groped about
to light the candles
and a fire
to keep me warm;
wondering how
men manage, who
have no fire, no candlelight
to company them
some stormy night.

*L*eave them quietly at His feet:
Day is past;
Bitter mingled with the sweet,
Dies are cast.
Reality surpassed the dreams,
Kindly, He overruled my schemes;
His truth, those tentative "it seems";
Heaven at last!

Blinking
back the tears
I'm thinking,
may just clear
the heart for sight;
as windshield wipers
help us
on a stormy,
windswept night.

$\mathscr{I}$f I lived within the sound
of the sea's relentless yearning,
my soul would rise and fly to seek
what the soul longs for—unable to speak;
aware, as I go, of Him everywhere:
in my heart, in the clouds . . . in the cold wet air . . .
And my soul would worship in joyful prayer,
receding as the waves recede,
returning with the waves' returning,
reaching up, as for Him, feeling,
then with the waves kneeling . . .
                                        kneeling . . .
                                                    kneeling . . .

God of the Universe
in power abiding,
whose Son both death endured
and death defied,
returning omnipresent
as before; confiding
all to You,
an irrevocable trust,
I find my leaden spirit
rising from the dust.
Confident that You,
Who've brought them
thus far on the way,
will see them through.

$\mathcal{I}$ awoke to a world
of whitening wonder:
all the bareness of
Winter landscape under
soft white snow
fallen . . .
. . . and still falling . . .
as the dusk falls.
The mountains 'round
are whited out, . . .
and still it falls,
leaving only the nearer woods
etched stark against
the white about.
The only color I can see:
a red bird in a whitened tree.
The only sound in a world gone still:
a towhee on my windowsill.

*L*eave them to God
those distant, sinister souls
whose crimes unmentionable
stained history's pages red,
decimated races,
searing minds of survivors;
leave them to God.
For there are those today
perpetrating crimes
as hideous as theirs,
unnoticed and unmentioned.
Only the past concerns.
What if, in satisfying vengeance,
we sacrifice the living
for the dead?
Divert attention from
the present holocaust?
Why must more die
while those who could help
remain in mental ghettos
of a time long gone?
Perhaps some evil force
would have it so.
And still they die.
Diversionary tactics?
Is that why?

*L*et them go—
the things that have
accumulated through the years.
If they are only things
then let them go.
Like barnacles
they but impede the ship
and slow it down
when it should go
full speed ahead.
Why dread
the disentangling?
Does the snake
mourn the shedding
of its skin?
When the butterfly escapes
its chrysalis,
does regret
set in?

It hangs there
like an evil thing,
this curve of iron
that 'round some slave's neck
curled and snapped . . .
the slave, long past,
his collar worn rib-thin,
rigid in rust
as if at last
its own rigor mortis
had set in.

The fledgling
eager to be free,
struggling
for liberty,
coming home
in later years,
found she came
in tears.

The other one,
nudged from the nest
(reluctantly,
to make her fly),
coming back
in later years,
found she could
not cry.

$\mathcal{I}$t is a fearful thing to fall
into Your hands, O living God!"
Yet I must trust him to You,
praying your staff and rod
will comfort him in need
as well as break,
in love, the wayward leg. And yet I plead,
"Deal gently with the young man
for my sake."

$\mathcal{M}$oses' wanderings weren't
all for naught:
wandering, he learned the
wilderness firsthand;
and later through this
"Devastation" brought
His brethren from bondage to
the Promised Land.

Hebrews 12:1

Compassed about
with a great cloud . . ."
the Scriptures say;
if only I could hear
one shout . . .
the distant roar
of that great crowd,
just some small word
aloud . . .
aloud . . .
to cheer my way.

$\mathcal{S}$unk in this gray
depression
I cannot pray.
How can I give
expression
when there're no words
to say?
This mass of vague
foreboding,
of aching care,
fear with its
overloading
short-circuits prayer.
Then in this fog
of tiredness,
this nothingness I find
only a quiet knowing
that He is kind.

$\mathcal{G}$od,
bless all young mothers
at end of day,
kneeling wearily with each
small one
to hear them pray.
Too tired to rise when done . . .
and yet, they do,
longing just to sleep
one whole night through.

Too tired to sleep . . .
too tired to pray . . .
God,
bless all young mothers
at close of day.

God rest you merry,
gentlemen . . ."
and in these pressured days
I, too, would seek to be so blessed
by Him, who still conveys
His merriment, along with rest.
So I would beg, on tired knees,
"God rest me merry,
please . . ."

He had returned, the prodigal.
The father,
from his long months of waiting,
flew down the path
to welcome him once more,
killing the fatted calf,
calling for robes and ring
as if not anything
had gone between . . . All as before.
The celebration had begun.
Then—
a gloom fell . . .
It was the older son
who knew the younger well.
The Father stood between
the sinful "was,"
the righteous "might have been."

There are few
who know a father's heart
can be so torn in two.

"Where can I go from your Spirit?"

*F*leeing from You,
  nothing he sees
  of Your preceding
  as he flees.

Choosing his own path
  how could he know
  Your hand directs
  where he shall go.

Thinking he's free,
  "free at last,"
  unaware Your right hand
  holds him fast.

Waiting for darkness
  to hide in night,
  not knowing, with You
  dark is as light.

Poor prodigal!
  Seeking a "where" from "whence"
  how does one escape
  omnipotence?

Cradle her within your arms
when evening falls
after the wearying day;
secure her in tenderness
that she may sleep
her tiredness away.
Passion is a gift from God,
but when the body aches
with weariness, one longs
for quiet love. It takes
so little to restore the soul,
so little to renew:
just gather her within your arms,
let her sleep close to you.

He fell on the sidewalk . . .
I saw him fall,
too drunk to walk
he could only crawl
to a scraggly tree
that grew near the street;
with the help of that tree
he got on his feet.

~

In my heart always,
God, help me see
he got on his feet
for . . .
there was a Tree!

Hebrews 1:3

Listen, Lord,
a mother's praying
low and quiet:
listen, please.
Listen what her tears
are saying,
see her heart
upon its knees;
lift the load
from her bowed shoulders
till she sees
and understands,
You, Who hold
the worlds together,
hold her problems
in Your hands.

Satan speaks:

𝓗erein
lies my cleverest ploy,
Hell's greatest power,
this plot
that fills me with Satanic joy
convincing those within our
jurisdiction, that somehow
I am not."

𝒯here has been wind
and earthquake, too;
followed by fire;
he stood, fearthinned,
encaved, to view
the holocaust expire.

Yet—
You were in none of these:
Your still small voice next,
—please.

From lack of simple gratitude
for simple things;
my self-encrusted attitude,
limp, lazy wings;
from the foul breath of bitterness
—the noble whine;
shackling Providence with my less,
Your choice with mine:
save me from each, for other's sake,
each loathsome trait, lest I become
trapped buglike in the web I make
of self-imposed, sweet martyrdom.

$\mathcal{D}$rifting . . .
Slipping . . .
slow I went,
no leap in sudden haste,
but quietly I eased away
into this silent waste.

How long it's been, I do not know;
a minute from Him seems
like long midnights of emptiness,
and silent screams.

I heard the distant promises
wistfully and groped to see
a glimmer of Him in the dark:
Could He see me?

There was no pounding on the Gates,
—no cry at Heaven's door,
I had no strength; my tears left
a puddle on the floor.

Then from my crumpled nothingness,
my dungeon of despair,
a quiet opening of the door
—a breath of Living Air.

He let me sleep—as if I'd died—
yet when the morning broke
the Risen Son discovered me,
and I awoke.

New I awoke; His warming love,
updrawing, transformed everything.
Tell me—
is this the way
An acorn feels
in Spring?

The harbor:
loaded freighters,
fishing boats, yachts, and such.
Yet—
as the lights
twinkle on, one by one,
in the quickening dusk—
my heart is with
one small sailboat
heading home.

*L*ord,
he whom Thou lovest
is ill,
and it is night.

Numb we wait
Thy will
helpless with fright.

(How can mere hours be
eternity?)

Slowly we know
before a word
is said:
Lord,
he whom Thou lovest
is dead.

$\mathcal{H}$e's not dead,
but we
struggling to live
upon this cursed earth
wearied by work,
not free,
to come and go at will
bound by gravity,
limitations of
our mere mortality.
Since he has broken thru
restrictions of this life,
entered There
eternally young, and free
of sin and sickness,
aging and the woes
that cramp and cripple us,
God, who are we
to moan and weep
when it is not he
but we
who sleep?

Giants they stood,
in the virgin wood.
And when
they were needed,
mountain men
felled them,
hewed and adzed them,
grooved and cut them,
hauled and built them;
Then there stood,
sturdy and small,
a simple mountain cabin
in the wood,
that was all
a mountain woman
wanted for her brood.
And when it was done
the man said,
"It is good."

What does one do
   with a wound left untended
When suddenly all that
   was honorable died
Leaving a numbness that
   grew till it ended
In pain unendurable. Tried
As she would, she could only
   stare tearlessly
Into a future fogged
   with a stench;
She who had faced life
   joyfully, fearlessly
Found herself stopped by
   this soul-shattering wrench.

$\mathcal{G}$ive me your nights,"
the quiet voice
of God said to my
pressured heart.
Wakeful and fretting
I knew I had the
choice:
For me the easy or
the better part?

Nights are for sleeping,
one of His kindest gifts
which, if He withholds
is for a special reason.
Some work the daylight,
some the midnight shifts.
Could nights become
for me a special season?

"Give me your nights";
His voice unheard
spoke again. And my heart,
sleepless, stirred,
listened in silence
then acquiesced.
For only in compliance
I am blessed.

This I offer, child of Mine—
A bitter and an aging cup,
no salvage in the odd design,
take it, take and drink it up.
I chose you, knowing as I did,
no other one whom I could trust
to drink it quietly as I did:
accepting, silently, a must.

$\mathcal{L}$ord,
bless your children;
hold them close,
who love
you least,
but need you
most.

I reach out through the dark
to touch your hand;
through driving rain
I strive in vain
to see your face;
please understand.
I called you
but the wind that blew and blew
dispelled my cry.
You never knew.

Were you feeling for me
through the dark
as I for you?
Did you search for my face
through pouring rain
as I searched, too?
Did gusting winds obliterate your voice?

I never knew.

*A*s I was praying
day and night,
night and day,
quietly God was saying
"Let there be light
—My way."

❧

It was a pale blue dawn
dewy
and still.
Three golden clouds
stretched thin
above the black hill.
The purpling coves
awash in mist
slowly turned
to amethyst.
It was a pale blue dawn . . .

Peace
came as suddenly today
as came the storm
a day ago.
My soul was drenched
in wind and rain
frozen in fear
that fell like snow.
Then all was still.
Had someone prayed?
I do not know.

The house was full of living then
And there was need to view
The quiet spreading of the hills
Heaven's vast expanse of blue.
This old house is empty now,
With mostly only me,
The trees are crowding up the hill
As if for company.
I would not have mine back for good.
My birds have learned to fly.
But I find lovely comfort when
A wild bird builds close by.

$\mathscr{A}$ little more time,
Lord,
just a little more time.
There's so much to do,
so much undone.
If it's all right with You,
Lord,
please stop the sun.
There's forever before me
forever with You;
but a little more time
for the so much to do.

There is this mist
that rolls between
my yearning
and the mountain scene.
Silent it swirls
through bush and tree
and cooly curls
till wrapped in white,
a living veil
is all I see;
its eerie light
turning earth pale.
Yet in my spirit's
dry despair,
thirsting to see
from here
to There
I think
this isn't fair.

Encased in silent white
my ear
alerts to sounds
it wouldn't hear
if all were clear;
the traffic's distant
muffled roar,
the songs of birds
I've heard before,
unhearing;
bunting, finches,
and tiny wren;
endearing
little hunger chirps
when
(ignoring me)
the mothers come
to feed their broods
choosing our porch
instead of woods.
The cricket,
which I had forgot
still chirping
in his same old spot.
How good, I thought,
that sometimes we
enclosed in mist
hear, more than see.

I lay my "whys?"
before Your cross
in worship kneeling,
my mind beyond all hope,
my heart beyond all feeling;
and worshipping,
realize that I
in knowing You,
don't need a "why?"

Satan trembles
when he sees
the weakest saint
upon his knees."
But Satan laughs
without restraints
when saints go clobbering
other saints.

$\mathcal{H}$e took His cross
as best he could
(cross-bearing was
so new to him.)
How could he tell
the torturous load
of rough hewn wood
on that rutted road
where he was led,
would saw his shoulder
till it bled?
and then . . .
he fell.

Of all the curious,
crowding round,
Who,
stepping out, stooped down
to do
what Simon did
long years ago,
—but He, Who
staggering beneath our cross
fell, too.

$\mathcal{T}$wo ways part now and I stand
   uncertain and perplexed.
Whither, Lord, next?

One friend says this, another that.
   I have no choice.
   Lord, for Thy voice.

But look! one path is stained with blood.
   Footprints I see.
   I follow Thee.

He died—
the thief—
and yet,
before,
he'd cried
for mercy
and, what's more,
his tortured soul
had found relief.

He got
a death
that he deserved;
a Life
that he did not.

Each man has his Isaac
(each lesser Abraham);
some "only son"
God says must die:
and so have I.
Yet all the time I wonder,
what if there is no ram?
No staying hand,
no quick reprieve,
to let mine live?

White flowers
in memory of her,
this year—
my first.
I'd thought
they'd bring a tear,
my heart would burst.
Yet flowers brought
a flood of memories
with which
my life
is full.
Because of her
I'm rich.

The long, gray winter
now is past—
the coldest we
have ever seen—
and I am glad
to note at last
earth's first bright
touch of green.

*T*hose
splendid, soaring
jagged peaks,
stripped of trees
of grass and sod
on whose snow
the sunlight lingers
are but the braille
letters, where we mortals
blind and fragile
trace our fingers
to spell the name
God.

A still day—
the sky grew dark,
(darkness fell, too,
at Calvary).
Thunder, like the wrath of God,
shook the earth—
as lightning split
the low hung clouds;
then came the rain.
Pelting those crowds
thronging,
singing,
longing—

It was still day
the world grew dark. Thunder
came with tanks and guns
a generation falling under
brute force. Lightning split
power from people.
Then came the rains
—to wash away
the stains?

*I*nto the heart of the Infinite can a mere mortal
    hope to gain access,
what with no part of me geared to His greatness,
to His vastness my infinite less?
Yet the longing for Him was so wide and so deep,
by day it crowded life's thronging,
by night it invaded my sleep

~

Then came the pain:
again . . .
    and again . . .
        and again . . .

~

As if a wing tip were brushing the tears
    from my face
for the breath of a second I knew the unknowable,
glimpsed invisible grace.

And I lay where for long in despair I had lain;
entered, unshod, the holy There where God
    dwells with His pain—
alone with the pain of the price He had paid
in giving His Son for a world gone astray
—the world He had made.

My heart lay in silence,
worshipped in silence;
and questioned no more.

NOTES

19 *Spare not the pain*—Fall of 1937, before leaving China for college

20 *Test me, Lord, and give me strength*—November 1937, aboard The U.S.S. Pres. McKinley on the way from China to college in the States

21 *Teach me contentment, Lord, whate'er my lot*—1937, first week at college

22 *Bravely the little bird clung there*—1938, college. When I saw it, it was a dried and shriveled thing hanging by a string that had got caught.

29 *As the portrait is unconscious*—Wheaton, 1940, Mother's Day. Portrait completed November 8, 1974

33 *You held my hand, and I*—October 24, 1942, sometime after meeting Bill

56 *The field that night was a sea of mud*—Montreat, North Carolina, September 16, 1944, World War II with R.M.

58 *"I'm Daniel Creasman's mother"*—Hinsdale, Illinois 1943, first funeral Bill conducted after our marriage

60 *Bless him, Lord, in leaving*—A group of young preachers we knew were gathered around talking when they mentioned one Asian student and how much he had sacrificed leaving a wife and six children at home, while he studied for his degree in America.

90 *Love without clinging*—Little Piney Cove, 1967, to a young bride

98 *Never turn your back on tears*—May 1971, advice to a new husband

102 *Death . . . death can be faced*—October 8, 1971, for the P.O.W. and M.I.A. wives

105 *Theirs is a still-less, restless grave*—Vero Beach, Florida, 1972. Spanish Galleons sank off the coast in the 1700's

114 *Perhaps she will land*—London, 1972, for W.S. She was a street kid when I first met her in a large city. After she told me of her early years, I understood her present life, and her

addiction to drugs. She was a baby Christian learning to walk, and like any baby learning to walk, she fell. And fell frequently. Her Christian life was one step forward, two steps back. Each fall was followed by repentance and a renewed effort to follow Jesus. Whenever I was in that city I looked her up. We wrote regularly. The last time I was in that city, many years had passed. Her once young, laughing face was drawn. Her sparkling brown eyes, tired. This was written for her.

133 *Low gray skies*—Washington, D.C., January 20, 1973, inauguration

134 *Of this historic moment*—Austin, Texas, January 25, 1973, L.B.J. funeral

135 *Larger than life he lived here*—L. B. J. Ranch Cemetery, January 25, 1973

143 *Atop the ridge*—Spring, 1973. They reminded me of how Daddy cared for Mother after her stroke.

194 *Beyond all custom all tradition*—The Murderer's Prayer, April 5, 1977

210 *Another lamb will join the fold*—Los Alamos, New Mexico, February 8, 1978, after Gigi called on her way to the hospital. In the early morning Stephan called to say Jerusha had arrived.

226 *Leave them to God*—January 6, 1980, after reading *Life* magazine

228 *It hangs there like an evil thing*—Little Piney Cove, September 20, 1978. The ancient iron slave collar from Jamaica hangs above my desk.

229 *The fledgling eager to be free*—Tsingkiang (now Huaiyin), Kiangsu, China, May 14, 1980

230 *It is a fearful thing to fall*—Hebrews 10:31, Psalm 23, 2 Samuel 18:5, Little Piney Cove, August 3, 1980

231 *Moses' wanderings weren't all for naught*—September 27, 1980

232 *Compassed about with a great cloud*—Hebrews 12:1, Minneapolis, October 22, 1980

233 *Sunk in this gray depression*—September 1980

234 *God, bless all young mothers*—Atlanta airport, November 23, 1980

235 *"God rest you merry, gentlemen"*—R.B.G., Christmas 1980

236 *He had returned, the prodigal*—December 22, 1980

237 *Fleeing from You, nothing he sees*—Luke 15 in light of Psalm 139:7–12, R.B.G.

INDEX OF FIRST LINES